Learn Simple

Free Gift Coupons

Learn	Learn	Learn
UI using	**IoT using**	**API using**
SAPUI5	**SAP HANA**	**SAP Gateway**
and be	and be	and be
In demand	**an Innovator**	**Awesome**

Grab it - it's yours !

You Might Be Also Interested In

Kindle Book Links

 Learn SAP® UI5: The new enterprise Javascript framework with examples

 SAP® Netweaver Gateway: Learn how to use SAP® Netweaver Gateway for UI5 and ABAP projects

 Data Visualization In 7 Simple Steps

 Learn D3.js Simple Way

Copyright © 2015 by UI5CN

Rua Aquilino Ribeiro L280,

Pontinha, Lisbon

1675-292 PT

+351-968621883

www.UI5CN.com

1. The main category of the book — COMPUTERS > Enterprise Applications > General

TECHNOLOGY & ENGINEERING.

2. Another subject category — Information Technology > Enterprise Software

First Edition

Content

Content   **4**

Preface   **6**

1. Introduction   **7**

    1.1 Real World   **9**

    1.2 IoT Enablement Factors   **11**

        1.2.1 Miniaturization of Devices   11

        1.2.2 Radio Frequency Identification (RFID)   11

        1.2.3 Internet Protocol Version 6 (IPv6)   11

        1.2.4 Communication Throughput and Lower Latency 12

        1.2.5 Low Power Consumption Devices   12

        1.2.6 Cloud Computing   12

        1.2.7 Improved Security and Privacy   13

    1.3 IoT Architecture   **14**

2. Getting Started with IoT Use Cases   **15**

    2.1 Open Hardware Platforms Will Help You Build Your Thing   **15**

    2.2 Learn About IoT Standards   **16**

    2.3 Get Out Of Comfort Zone!   **17**

    2.4 Follow Your End To End Tutorial   **18**

3. Project: SAP HANA Internet of Things (IoT): Raspberry PI, Arduino Uno, XSJS &SAPUI5   **19**

    3.1 Introduction to the Project   **19**

3.2 Introduction to Arduino Uno And Raspeberry Pi 21

3.3 Setting Up Arduino Uno 25

3.4 Setting Up Raspberry Pi 32

3.5 Setting Up Java Program To Read Serial Port 45

3.6 Setting Up SAP Hana Using Native Development 53

3.7 Setting Up SAPUI5 64

3.8 Tying Loose Ends and Going Live 79

4. Bonus 81

Preface

Change has always been and will be the key component of progress. All change is hard at first, messy in the middle but gorgeous in the last. In this book, we are going to show the journey and the steps we went through to achieve something that is changing the world.

Internet of Things needs no introduction. It is the capability of connecting real life objects to enable them to achieve greater value and service by exchanging data and information. As per Forbes, this is now the most talked technology, beating big data (dated May 2015) and this is not a temporary hype, but the beginning of an era, which will stay for the next 5-10 years.

Internet of Things is not a new radical concept that just came into existence now but in reality, it is a capability that is possible only now, due to the advances in database technology like SAP HANA, increased bandwidth, reduced size, and power consumption of devices.

Few years back, we started testing the waters by looking into different ways in which we could connect different components, in order to create a basic use-case application of Internet of Things. It looked like a quadratic equation with many solutions but to reduce the complexity we stick to KISS principle and kept it simple to bring together all the information required to get started, in no time.

1. Introduction

The IOT concept was initially coined by a member of the Radio Frequency Identification (RFID) development community in 1999, and it has recently become more relevant to the practical world largely because of the growth of mobile devices, embedded and ubiquitous communication, cloud computing and data analytics.

Since then, many have seized on the phrase "Internet of Things" to refer to the general idea of things, especially everyday objects, that are readable, recognisable, locatable, addressable, and/or controllable via the Internet, irrespective of the communication means (whether via RFID, wireless LAN, wide- area networks, or other means).

Everyday objects include not only the electronic devices we encounter or the products of higher technological development such as vehicles and equipment but things that we do not ordinarily think of as electronic at all - such as food and clothing.

Examples of "things" include:

- People

- Animals and Natural ecosystem

- Location (of objects)

- Time Information (of objects)

- Condition (of objects)

These "things" of the real world shall seamlessly integrate into the virtual world, enabling anytime, anywhere connectivity.

In 2010, the number of everyday physical objects and devices connected to the Internet was around 1 billion.

Cisco forecasts that this figure will reach to 25 billion in 2015 as the number of more smart devices per person increases, and to a further 50 billion by 2020.

In addition, the global economic impact, which IoT will collectively have, will be more than $14 Trillion; if we compare this to the world population, then by 2020 we will have around more than six connected devices per person.

1.1   Real World

In today's IT industry, companies are staying competitive by adopting new technologies, streamlining business processes and innovating new services to increase productivity and save costs.

In the logistics and supply chain, the traditional supply of goods is based on established agreements between manufacturers and suppliers. Orders are made in advance and various stakeholders in the supply chain, i.e., assembly lines, manufacturers, and logistics managers, do the tracking.

With the use of smart technologies such as active RFID (executable codes in tag), it is possible to envision that goods may be transported without human intervention from manufacturers to suppliers.

Warehouses will become completely automatic with goods moving in and out; forwarding of the goods will be made, using intelligent decisions based on information received via readers and positioning systems to optimise transiting routes.

Suppliers will have the flexibility to purchase parts from various manufacturers (possibly from competing manufacturers) and buy them in a sequence of individual orders.

Such automation creates a dynamic production and transportation network and provides better asset management to improve the overall efficiency in the supply chain.

In healthcare, hospitals are shifting from providing healthcare on premise, i.e., in hospitals and clinics, to remote self-monitoring for patients.

Self-monitoring benefits patients by giving them greater freedom and independence in monitoring their health and frees up hospital equipment for the treatment of emergencies.

IoT will have a huge impact in environmental regulation and control as well where we will be able to monitor and control the global problem of clean air, global warming and recycling.

It will also provide a connected world where private transportation can talk to each other in order to create an accident free scenario and the best experience for consumers, taking care of medical and emotional need while transit.

Manufacturer will be able to collect valuable information by opening a two way channel to customers which will radical increase the chance of improvement and reduce the risk of failure of consumer goods.

Factories will be able to run in more robust and self-sustain way using so called Industry 4.0.

1.2   IoT Enablement Factors

1.2.1 Miniaturization of Devices

The size (and cost) of electronic components that are needed to support capabilities such as sensing, tracking and control has been reducing and will continue to reduce as per Moore's law.

1.2.2 Radio Frequency Identification (RFID)

Moving into the future, RFID has the potential to provide streams of data that will provide information systems with real-time, item-specific data and be flexible enough to be placed in extremely small spaces and locations, i.e., coil-on-chip technology.

1.2.3 Internet Protocol Version 6 (IPv6)

IPv6 is the next Internet addressing protocol that is used to replace IPv4. With IPv6, there are approximately 3.4×1038 (340 trillion) unique IPv6 addresses, allowing the Internet to continue to grow and innovate.

1.2.4 Communication Throughput and Lower Latency

Low latency makes it possible for IOT applications to query or receive quicker updates from sensor devices. LTE networks have latencies about 50-75 ms, which will open up new types of programming possibilities for application developers.

1.2.5 Low Power Consumption Devices

Low Power consumption devices will allow the devices to run for longer duration. Some devices will use solar capability to run, which will be self-sustained.

1.2.6 Cloud Computing

IOT connects billions of devices and sensors to create new and innovative applications. In order to support these applications, a reliable, elastic, and agile platform is essential. Cloud computing is one of the enabling platforms to support IOT, which provides required storage, processing power, and scaling capability.

1.2.7 Improved Security and Privacy

This allows the communication channel to be trustworthy. Critical business data can be passed by encryption or authentication code

(MAC), protecting the confidentiality and authenticity of transaction data as it "transits" between networks.

There is still evolving standards in IoT security and with IPv6, IPsec support is integrated into the protocol design and connections can be secured when communicating with other IPv6 devices.

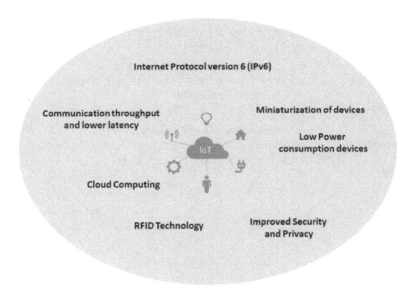

1.3 IoT Architecture

IOT architecture consists of different suite of technologies supporting IOT. It serves to illustrate how various technologies relate to each other and to communicate the scalability, modularity and configuration of IOT deployments in different scenarios. The functionality of each layer is described below:

Application Layer:
Enable user to interact and provide the user experience for the system(s)

Management Service:
Enable processing of information through analytics, security controls, process modeling and management of devices

Gateway Layer:
Enable robust and high performance wired or wireless network infrastructure as a transport medium

Sensor connectivity and Network:
Enable the interconnection of the physical and digital worlds allowing real-time information to be collected and processed

You can also check our SAP HANA Internet of Things(IoT) video course for accelerated learning: here or use the below QR code.

SAP HANA Internet of Things(IoT):Raspberry, Uno, PubNub, UI5

UI5 Community Network • SAP Experts - SAP Services, SAP Consulting, SAP Education

★ ★ ★ ★ ★ 4.2 (40 ratings) • 29 lectures • 4.5 hours video • All Levels

2. Getting Started with IoT Use Cases

Now coming to the fun stuff on how you, as a developer or technical consultant, can start. There are few very basic advices that we can follow:

2.1   Open Hardware Platforms Will Help You Build Your Thing

It's amazing to see that only a few years back, it was virtually impossible for someone to have access to actual hardware to run IoT solutions. That is, cheap and reasonably sized equipment that you could easily deploy in a house or car.

Nowadays, platforms like Arduino, Intel Edison board, BeagleBone and Raspberry Pi are providing IoT developers with a wide ecosystem of hardware that can be used to easily prototype and even go to production for small batches.

2.2   Learn About IoT Standards

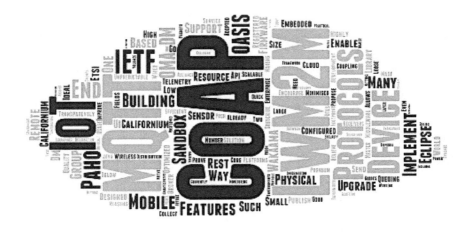

source : eclipse.org

What is really interesting in the Internet of Things space is that we're talking about millions of devices that are pretty limited in terms of processing power and communication capabilities.

Think of a tiny battery-powered microcontroller, monitoring a solar panel in the middle of the Death Valley!

And yet, one needs reliable ways to access sensor data or manage the software running in the device, all of this, usually happening over the air and with limited human intervention.
While the term IoT is new, the use cases we see today have been around for several years, and there are interesting open standards that help build interoperable, efficient IoT solutions.

In order to allow IoT data to flow from producers (sensors on the field) to consumers (IT backends, web apps, etc.), there is **MQTT**, an

OASIS standard that implements a publish-subscribe communication model.

It has several QoS levels making it easy to find the perfect tradeoff between reliability and resources/bandwidth usage.

You should definitely read the MQTT 3.1.1 specification document to get more familiar with the protocol, and see by yourself that it is indeed a simple and interesting protocol for IoT.

OMA Lightweight M2M is another interesting standard from the Open Mobile Alliance that is getting a lot of attention in the domain of Device Management.

LwM2M is proposing a standard way to do things like: reboot a device, install a new software image (yes, similarly to what happens on your smartphone and that is based on an ancestor of LwM2M called OMA-DM), etc.

At the transport level, Lightweight M2M is using CoAP (Constrained Application Protocol), which is an IETF standard targeting very constrained environments in which it's still desirable to have the kind of features you would expect from HTTP, in particular the manipulation of resources that you can "GET", "PUT", store in a local cache, etc.

2.3 Get Out Of Comfort Zone!

IoT is an incredible opportunity for all developers to learn about new technologies.

If you are used to developing backend applications, you will learn a lot about embedded development if you start playing with embedded runtimes like Contiki.

Being closer to the silicon means having to think about how to optimize radio communications, power consumption, etc., and this is truly fascinating.

If you are more into embedded development, then start experimenting with the various cloud services (time series databases, IoT brokers) you can connect your embedded system to, and learn how to turn your IoT data into something useful.

2.4   Follow Your End To End Tutorial

In addition, one of the important factors in making an IoT demo is to understand the basic skeleton of the project and start with the minimal configuration and then you can add on to the setup, to make it more production ready.

In the next section, we will start building a small end-to-end use case on IoT using Raspberry Pi, Arduino, sensor circuits and using SAP HANA XS as backend, which is exposed via REST based services.

You can also check our SAP HANA Internet of Things(IoT) video course for accelerated learning: here or use the below QR code.

 SAP HANA Internet of Things(IoT):Raspberry, Uno, PubNub, UI5

UI5 Community Network • SAP Experts - SAP Services. SAP Consulting. SAP Education

★ ★ ★ ★ ★ 4.2 (40 ratings) • 29 lectures • 4.5 hours video • All Levels

3. Project: SAP HANA Internet of Things (IoT): Raspberry PI, Arduino Uno, XSJS &SAPUI5

3.1   Introduction to the Project

Change has always been and will be the key component of progress. All change is hard at first, messy in the middle but gorgeous in the end.

In the following sections, we are going to show the journey and the steps we went through to achieve out IoT end-to-end use case.

Six months back, we started testing the waters by looking into different ways in which we could connect different components, in order to create a basic use-case application of Internet of Things.

Internet of Things is not a new radical concept that just came into existence now but in reality, it is a capability that is possible only now, due to the advances in database technology like SAP HANA and due to the capability to do complex operations on huge datasets in a blink of an eye.

So coming back to our use-case for Internet of Things, which we are going to cover now, we have selected a smart home example that will monitor our house; it is an example that everyone can relate to.

In the setup, we have a photo sensor that is connected to our Arduino Uno that reads the analogue data and sends it to Raspberry Pi, via serial communication.

There is a Java program running in the Raspberry Pi that reads the data from the serial port and, if there is a change, it sends the data to SAP HANA by XSJS calls.

On the frontend side, we have an SAPUI5 application that will show the readings, in real-time, in some nice tiles.

Let us see how we achieved this setup:

- Part 1: Introduction to Arduino, Raspberry Pi and why we have selected them
- Part 2: Setting up Arduino Uno
- Part 3: Setting up Raspberry Pi
- Part 4: Setting up Java Program to read serial port in Raspberry Pi
- Part 5: Setting up SAP HANA using Native development
- Part 6: Setting up SAP UI5
- Part 7: Go-Live

3.2 Introduction to Arduino Uno And Raspeberry Pi

Before starting the project, we should know why we have selected both Arduino Uno and Raspberry Pi.

Why Raspberry Pi?

The Raspberry Pi is a **low-cost credit-card-size computer** with an ARM-processor that has a huge community to help to build applications.

Raspberry Pi can **multitask processes** – it can run multiple programs in the background while activated; for example, you can have a Raspberry Pi that is serving as both a print server and a VPN server, at the same time.

Why Arduino?

Arduino is a **micro-controller** with easier capability to integrate analogue input. The Arduino IDE is significantly easier to use than Linux.

For example, if you wanted to write a program to blink a LED, with Raspberry Pi you would need to install an operating system and some code libraries – and that is just to start.

Whereas with Arduino, you can get a LED light to blink in just eight lines of code.

Arduino isn't designed to run an OS or a lot of software; you can just plug it in and get started.

You can leave an Arduino plugged in as it conducts a single process for a long time, and just unplug it when you're not using it. This is why we recommend the Arduino for beginners before going for Pi.

As per Limor Fried, the founder of Adafruit**,** a DIY electronics store that offers parts and kits for both Arduino and Pi projects, *"The Arduino is simpler, harder to 'break' or 'damage' and has much more learning resources at this time for beginners; with the Pi you have to learn some Linux as well as programming—such as Python. The Arduino works with any computer and can run off a battery. You can also turn it on and off, safely at any time. The Pi setup can be damaged by unplugging it without a proper shutdown."*

While the **Raspberry Pi shines in software application**, the **Arduino makes hardware projects very simple**. It's simply a matter of figuring out what you want to do.
Sound like Raspberry Pi is superior to Arduino, but that's only when it comes to **software applications**. Arduino's simplicity makes it a much better bet for **pure hardware projects**.

The ultimate answer when deciding between the Pi and Arduino is, "Why choose?"

If you are looking to learn about IoT, each one will teach you something different.

Raspberry Pi and Arduino are complementary. Ideally, expert suggests a scenario where the Arduino is the sensory workhouse, while the Pi doles out directions.

Our SAP HANA IoT Project Steps

Therefore, we are going to do exactly that, in the following sections we are going to use:

1. Arduino for analogue interface
2. and providing data in digital format to Raspberry Pi
3. and Pi should take care of communication to SAP HANA

Simplified steps are:

Step 1: Connect **Arduino to a Computer** and checking if the analogue input is working perfectly. For this experiment, we have photo sensors that will detect light intensity and give the data to a computer by serial port communication, through Arduino.

Step 2: **Connect Raspberry Pi to Arduino** and able to establish the same configuration, which was achieved via computer and Arduino. Also, setting up a webserver in Raspberry Pi that can communicate over internet.

Step 3: Storing data into the SAP HANA system from Pi and **displaying it using SAPUI5** in near real time.

3.3   Setting Up Arduino Uno

In this section, we will connect our Arduino to a computer and checking if the analogue input is working perfectly.

For this experiment, we have photo sensors that will detect the light intensity and give the data to a computer by serial port communication.

First, install the Arduino Kit from http://www.arduino.cc/en/Main/Software, to your computer; in our scenario, we will be using Windows.

It looks like this, after the installation:

Check also the serial port that is connected to Arduino and set the right port in your installed software:

Now, for this demo we are going to follow the circuit in this diagram:

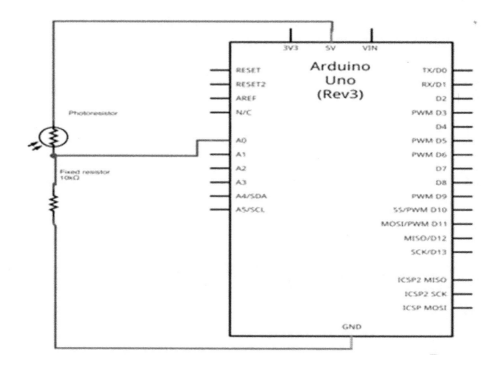

Our circuit looks like this:

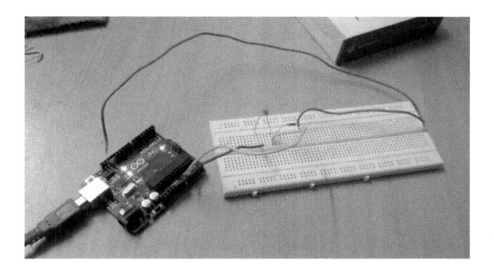

Let us have a look at the code that takes analogue input from serial output:

```
1.    /*
2.
3.    Analog input, analog output, serial output
4.    Reads an analog input pin, maps the result to a range from
      0 to 255
5.    and uses the result to set the pulsewidth modulation (PWM)
      of an output pin.
6.    Also prints the results to the serial monitor.
7.    The circuit:
8.    * potentiometer connected to analog pin 0.
9.    Center pin of the potentiometer goes to the analog pin.
10.   side pins of the potentiometer go to +5V and ground
11.   * LED connected from digital pin 9 to ground
12.   created 29 Dec. 2008
13.   modified 9 Apr 2012
```

```
14.    by Tom Igoe
15.    This example code is in the public domain.
16.    */
17.    // These constants won't change. They're used to give
       names
18.    // to the pins used:
19.    const int analogInPin = A0; // Analog input pin that the
       potentiometer is attached to
20.    const int analogOutPin = 9; // Analog output pin that the
       LED is attached to
21.    int sensorValue = 0; // value read from the pot
22.    int outputValue = 0; // value output to the PWM (analog
       out)
23.    void setup() {
24.    // initialize serial communications at 9600 bps:
25.    Serial.begin(9600);
26.    }
27.    void loop() {
28.    // read the analog in value:
29.    sensorValue = analogRead(analogInPin);
30.    // map it to the range of the analog out:
31.    outputValue = map(sensorValue, 0, 1023, 0, 255);
32.    // change the analog out value:
33.    analogWrite(analogOutPin, outputValue);
34.    // print the results to the serial monitor:
35.    Serial.println(sensorValue);
36.    // wait 5 milliseconds before the next loop
37.    // for the analog-to-digital converter to settle
38.    // after the last reading:
39.    delay(500);
40.    }
```

Here we are trying to read the analogue signal from the photo sensor, via Arduino, and then Arduino will send it via serial port to the computer and use it to show the sensor data readings.

After writing the program, you should upload the program to the Arduino Uno.

And now to see the magic happening, open the serial monitor in top right side of the program.

We have demonstrated the result in this video: SAP HANA IoT with Arduino and Raspberry Pi.

QR code for the link:

3.4   Setting Up Raspberry Pi

In this section, we will connect Raspberry Pi to Arduino and able to establish the same configuration which was achieved via computer and Arduino.

Here, we are going to do the Raspberry Pi configuration and connecting it to the Arduino Uno.

Raspberry Pi is capable of running a complete operating system and the real advantage is the capability to running with so less power consumption and the easiness to interface with other micro-controllers and digital/analogue devices.

Why do we use Arduino here?

Raspberry Pi is a fine little computer board, though not nearly as good as the Arduino when it comes to I/O capabilities.

Since our experiment has a sensor network setup, it will be simpler to interface it with Arduino Uno.

Once we have the Arduino connection setup, then we can connect

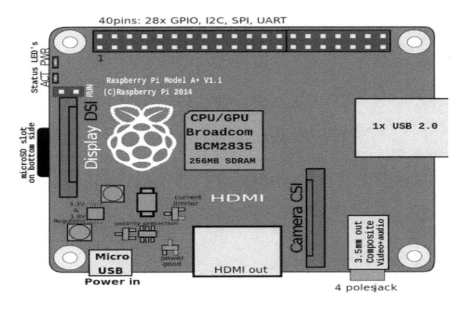

the Raspberry Pi through serial connection and do wonders with it.

Now, we are going to see how you can setup the connection of Raspberry and Arduino Uno in 10 simple steps:

Step 1: Download the RASPBIAN OS in Raspberry download section.

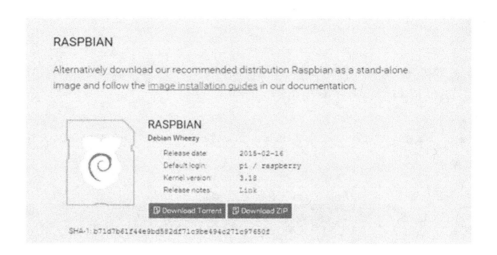

Step 2: Write the image to the disc (SD card) using Win32 image. Bear in mind that if you copy and paste the disk to image then it will

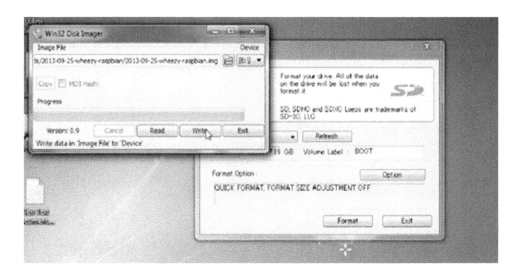

not work.

Step 3: Open the SD card in your computer and add the following line to the end of file *cmdline.txt*. Make sure that you leave a line break at the end, as in Linux it will be assumed to be execution of the command. It will be better to use *notepad++* to edit, as sometimes *notepad* can insert some windows specific characters in the file, which will not work in Linux (Raspberry system).

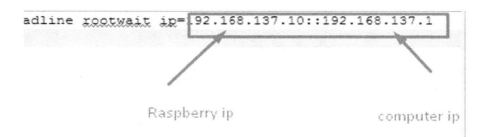

In the above image, the Raspberry IP address is the first one and our Ethernet port IP is the second one. This will enable to connect Raspberry Pi to the Internet through our computer.

Step 4: Change the IP of your Ethernet port to the IP, which you have specified in the config. file. In this tutorial, it is 192.168.137.1

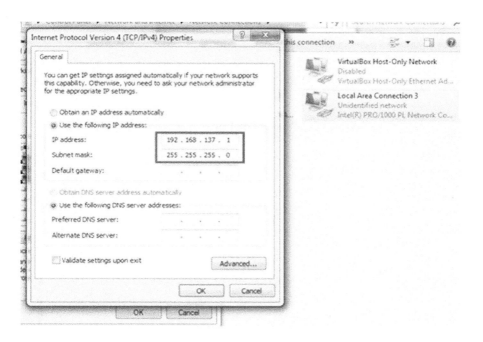

Step 5: Install *Xming* and *Putty*. *Putty* will be used to establish a SSH connection to Raspberry Pi and *Xming* will be used to create a graphical session. Download here the link of Putty and Xming.

Step 6: Once you have installed them, run Xming server and then open Putty.

Enter the IP address of the Raspberry Pi you configured in step 3, i.e. **192.168.137.10**

Also, make sure that you have SSH enabled in X11:

Now press open.

Step 7: It will ask for a user name and password: username is **pi** and password is **raspberry**

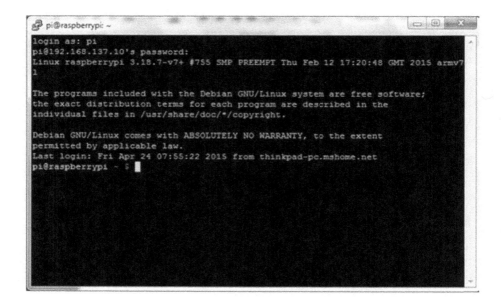

Now you are inside the Raspberry Pi.

To view the graphical interface, you have to type **lxsession** and if everything is correct, you will be able to see the graphical navigation window of Raspberry:

Step 8: After you have closed the graphical session using **CTR+ Z,** install Arduino to Raspberry, using the bellow commands:

```
sudo apt-get update
sudo apt-get install Arduino
```

After the installation, you will get a success message as well.

```
Ign http://raspberrypi.collabora.com wheezy/rpi Translation-en
Get:4 http://mirrordirector.raspbian.org wheezy/contrib armhf Packages [23.6 kB]
Get:5 http://mirrordirector.raspbian.org wheezy/non-free armhf Packages [49.3 kB]
]
Get:6 http://mirrordirector.raspbian.org wheezy/rpi armhf Packages [592 B]
Ign http://mirrordirector.raspbian.org wheezy/contrib Translation-en_GB
Ign http://mirrordirector.raspbian.org wheezy/contrib Translation-en
Ign http://mirrordirector.raspbian.org wheezy/main Translation-en_GB
Ign http://mirrordirector.raspbian.org wheezy/main Translation-en
Ign http://mirrordirector.raspbian.org wheezy/non-free Translation-en_GB
Ign http://mirrordirector.raspbian.org wheezy/non-free Translation-en
Ign http://mirrordirector.raspbian.org wheezy/rpi Translation-en_GB
Ign http://mirrordirector.raspbian.org wheezy/rpi Translation-en
Fetched 6,992 kB in 25s (277 kB/s)
Reading package lists... Done
pi@raspberrypi ~ $ $ sudo apt-get install arduino
-bash: $: command not found
pi@raspberrypi ~ $ sudo apt-get install arduino
Reading package lists... Done
Building dependency tree
Reading state information... Done
arduino is already the newest version.
0 upgraded, 0 newly installed, 0 to remove and 67 not upgraded.
pi@raspberrypi ~ $
```

Step 9: Open the graphical session again using **lxsession** command and open the Arduino sketch IDE that has been installed:

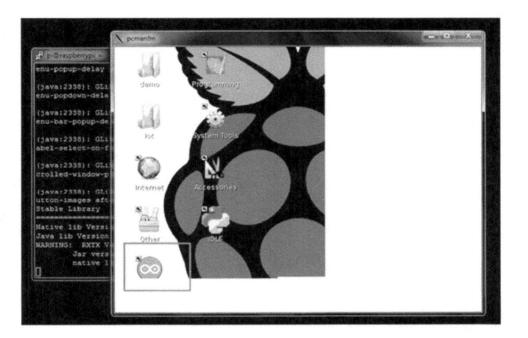

Step 10: Now we have the Arduino's sketch installed in the Raspberry Pi OS. This final step is to check if we can see the serial port connection visible (**/dev/ttyACM0** in Raspberry OS).

We will use port **/dev/ttyACM0** for our devices' communication, in the use cases.

3.5   Setting Up Java Program To Read Serial Port

In this section, we will use Java in Raspberry Pi in order to read serial data of Arduino

This part is the most challenging part for someone who is new to Raspberry Pi, so we have decided to create the entire setup in the utmost simplistic way in five sub-steps:

Step 1: Install java in the Raspberry Pi.

Usually Raspbian comes with Java installed but you can still check it via the following command:

```
java -version
```

When you update your Raspbian, it will also update the Java library, if required.

```
sudo apt-get update
```

Step 2: The communication is in serial mode, between Arduino and Raspberry Pi, so we need a way to make our Java program to understand it.

So download the below files:

- libjawt.so from here
- librxtxSerial.so from here
- RXTXcomm.jar from here

(if you are reading it in printed version please use the free digital version to reach the link or visit UI5CN.com)

and go to the download folder of the files and type the below commands; it will place all the necessary files in the appropriate folder to allow the serial communication from Raspberry Pi and Arduino:

```
sudo cp libjawt.so /usr/lib/jvm/jdk-8-oracle-arm-vfp-
hflt/lib/arm
sudo cp RXTXcomm.jar /usr/lib/jvm/jdk-8-oracle-arm-vfp-
hflt/jre/lib
sudo cp librxtxSerial.so /usr/lib/jvm/jdk-8-oracle-arm-vfp-
hflt/lib/arm
sudo cp librxtxSerial.so /usr/lib/jni/
```

Now, we are assuming here that you have your **jdk-8-oracle-arm-vfp-hflt** inside your **/usr/lib/jvm**. If you don't, then your Java won't be updated to jdk-8 and you have to update the JDK and JRE.

```
sudo apt-get install oracle-java8-installer
```

Step 3: Now you can copy below Java code.

```
1.    import java.io.BufferedReader;
2.    import java.io.InputStreamReader;
3.    import java.io.OutputStream;
4.    import gnu.io.CommPortIdentifier;
5.    import gnu.io.SerialPort;
6.    import gnu.io.SerialPortEvent;
7.    import gnu.io.SerialPortEventListener;
8.    import java.util.Enumeration;
9.    import java.net.HttpURLConnection;
10.   import java.net.URL;
11.
12.   public class SerialTestGET implements
      SerialPortEventListener {
13.   SerialPort serialPort;
14.   static int sensorValue = 0;
15.   /** The port we're normally going to use. */
16.   private static final String PORT_NAMES[] = {
17.   "/dev/tty.usbserial-A9007UX1", // Mac OS X
18.   "/dev/ttyACM0", // Raspberry Pi
19.   "/dev/ttyUSB0", // Linux
20.   "COM3", // Windows
21.   };
22.   /**
23.   * A BufferedReader which will be fed by a
      InputStreamReader
24.   * converting the bytes into characters
25.   * making the displayed results codepage independent
26.   */
27.   private BufferedReader input;
28.   /** The output stream to the port */
29.   private OutputStream output;
30.   /** Milliseconds to block while waiting for port open */
31.   private static final int TIME_OUT = 2000;
32.   /** Default bits per second for COM port. */
33.   private static final int DATA_RATE = 9600;
34.
35.   public void initialize() {
36.   // the next line is for Raspberry Pi and
```

```
37.   // gets us into the while loop and was suggested here was
      suggested
      http://www.raspberrypi.org/phpBB3/viewtopic.php?f=81&t=321
      86
38.   System.setProperty("gnu.io.rxtx.SerialPorts",
      "/dev/ttyACM0");
39.
40.   CommPortIdentifier portId = null;
41.   Enumeration portEnum =
      CommPortIdentifier.getPortIdentifiers();
42.
43.   //First, Find an instance of serial port as set in
      PORT_NAMES.
44.   while (portEnum.hasMoreElements()) {
45.   CommPortIdentifier currPortId = (CommPortIdentifier)
      portEnum.nextElement();
46.   for (String portName : PORT_NAMES) {
47.   if (currPortId.getName().equals(portName)) {
48.   portId = currPortId;
49.   break;
50.   }
51.   }
52.   }
53.   if (portId == null) {
54.   System.out.println("Could not find COM port.");
55.   return;
56.   }
57.
58.   try {
59.   // open serial port, and use class name for the appName.
60.   serialPort = (SerialPort)
      portId.open(this.getClass().getName(),
61.   TIME_OUT);
62.
63.   // set port parameters
64.   serialPort.setSerialPortParams(DATA_RATE,
65.   SerialPort.DATABITS_8,
66.   SerialPort.STOPBITS_1,
67.   SerialPort.PARITY_NONE);
68.
69.   // open the streams
```

```
70.   input = new BufferedReader(new
      InputStreamReader(serialPort.getInputStream()));
71.   output = serialPort.getOutputStream();
72.
73.   // add event listeners
74.   serialPort.addEventListener(this);
75.   serialPort.notifyOnDataAvailable(true);
76.   } catch (Exception e) {
77.   System.err.println(e.toString());
78.   }
79.   }
80.
81.   /**
82.   * This should be called when you stop using the port.
83.   * This will prevent port locking on platforms like Linux.
84.   */
85.   public synchronized void close() {
86.   if (serialPort != null) {
87.   serialPort.removeEventListener();
88.   serialPort.close();
89.   }
90.   }
91.
92.   /**
93.   * Handle an event on the serial port. Read the data and
      print it.
94.   */
95.   public synchronized void serialEvent(SerialPortEvent
      oEvent) {
96.   if (oEvent.getEventType() ==
      SerialPortEvent.DATA_AVAILABLE) {
97.   try {
98.   String inputLine=input.readLine();
99.   //System.out.println(inputLine);
100.  sendGet(inputLine);
101.  } catch (Exception e) {
102.  System.err.println(e.toString());
103.  serialPort.removeEventListener();
104.  serialPort.close();
105.  }
106.  }
```

```
107.    // Ignore all the other eventTypes, but you should
        consider the other ones.
108.    }
109.
110.    // HTTP GET request
111.    public void sendGet(String inputLine) throws Exception {
112.
113.    try{
114.    //if difference is more than 3 then send data to SAP HANA
115.    if(inputLine != null && inputLine .length() > 0 &&
        Math.abs(sensorValue - Integer.parseInt(inputLine)) > 3 ){
116.
117.    sensorValue = Integer.parseInt(inputLine);
118.    //Considering that A001 sensor is connection with this
        raspberry pie for now
119.    //we can even pass this with command line but for
        simplicityhardcoding it
120.    //Replace with your HANA server URL and port number
121.    String url =
        "http:///demoApp/demo01/app01/services/putSensorReading.xs
        js?id=A001&value=";
122.    url = url + inputLine;
123.
124.    URL obj = new URL(url);
125.    HttpURLConnection con = (HttpURLConnection)
        obj.openConnection();
126.
127.    // optional default is GET
128.    con.setRequestMethod("GET");
129.
130.    //add request header
131.    //con.setRequestProperty("User-Agent", USER_AGENT);
132.
133.    int responseCode = con.getResponseCode();
134.    if(responseCode == 200){
135.    System.out.println("OK value:"+inputLine);
136.    }else{
137.    System.out.println("Error: Response code "+responseCode);
138.    }
139.
140.    }
```

```
141.  System.out.println("OK value: Less than 3");
142.  }catch (Exception e) {
143.  System.err.println(e.toString());
144.  serialPort.removeEventListener();
145.  serialPort.close();
146.  }
147.
148.  }
149.
150.  public static void main(String[] args) throws Exception {
151.  SerialTestGET main = new SerialTestGET();
152.  main.initialize();
153.
154.  Thread t=new Thread() {
155.  public void run() {
156.  //the following line will keep this app alive for 1000
      seconds,
157.  //waiting for events to occur and responding to them
      (printing incoming messages to console).
158.  try {Thread.sleep(1000000);} catch (InterruptedException
      ie) {}
159.  }
160.  };
161.  t.start();
162.  System.out.println("Started");
163.  }
164.  }
```

Step 4: Compile it using below command:

```
javac -source 1.6 -target 1.6 -cp /usr/lib/jvm/jdk-8-oracle-
arm-vfp-hflt/jre/lib/RXTXcomm.jar SerialTestGET.java
```

Here, we are giving a class path of our *RXTX.jar* file and using 1.6
compatible compiler mode because the Jar file is 1.6 compatible.

Step 5: If there is no error (warnings may come), then your setup is right and you can now read the Arduino data in your serial port of Raspberry Pi, with the step 4 Java compiled code.

You can change the Java code of Step 3 and recompile it, in order to fit your requirements as well.

3.6   Setting Up SAP Hana Using Native Development

We have already covered all the steps related to hardware setup and configuration.

Now we will focus our attention on SAP HANA and interfacing it with our SAPUI5 frontend.

We will follow these steps for configuring SAP HANA:

Step1: Create the Data Definition for our **HANA XS**, which will be storing the data.

Step2: Create the **SQL procedures** to do data operations.

Step3: Create the XSJS services to act as a Gateway between the SQL Procedures calls and the **service calls for Raspberry Pi and SAPUI5 application**.

Step1: Create the Data Definition for HANA XS

We are going to name it *Demo Schema .hdbschema*.

Note here that demoApp.demo01.app02 is the package path and SHIOT_02 is the project name:

```
1.    namespace demoApp.demo01.app02.SHIOT_02.Data;
2.
3.    @Schema: 'DemoSchema'
4.
5.    context demo02sensorNetwork {
6.
7.    type sensor_key : String(10);
8.
9.    @Schema: 'DemoSchema'
10.
11.   context demo02sensorNetwork {
12.
13.   type sensor_key : String(10);
14.
15.   @Catalog.tableType : #COLUMN
16.
17.   Entity demo02sensor_info_MD {
18.
19.   key ID: sensor_key;
20.
21.   DESC: String(200);
22.
23.   };
24.
25.   @Catalog.tableType : #COLUMN
26.
27.   Entity demo02sensor_active_TS {
28.
29.   key ID: sensor_key;
30.
31.   key time_stamp: UTCTimestamp;
```

```
32.
33.    value : Integer;
34.
35.    };
```

Once you have activated the code, you need to create two tables:
demo02sensor_active_TS and demo02sensor_info_MD.

demo02sensor_active_TS: Stores the transactional Data of the sensors (readings with timestamp).

demo02sensor_info_MD: Stores the Master Data of the sensors (Sensor Id's)

Step2: Create the SQL procedures to do data operations

We have to create two SQL procedures for data operations:
insert_sensor_reading.hdbprocedure and
sensor_read.hdbprocedure.

As the names suggest, the first one is going to insert sensor data in sensor table and second one is going to read the recent sensor data from the table.

insert_sensor_reading.hdbprocedure is inside the folder Procedures.

It is taking sensor ID and sensor reading as input:

PROCEDURE

```
1.   "DemoSchema"."demoApp.demo01.app02.SHIOT_02.Procedures::in
     sert_sensor_reading" (
2.
3.   IN SENSORID NVARCHAR(10),
4.
5.   IN sensor_reading INTEGER )
6.
7.   LANGUAGE SQLSCRIPT AS
8.
9.   BEGIN
10.
11.  /****************************
12.
13.  Inserting sensor Data
14.
15.  ****************************/
16.
17.  insert into
     "demoApp.demo01.app02.SHIOT_02.Data::demos02sensorNetwork.
     demo02sensor_active_TS"
18.
19.  VALUES(:SENSORID, CURRENT_TIMESTAMP , sensor_reading
20.
21.  );
22.
23.  END;
```

`sensor_read.hdbprocedure` is inside the folder Procedures.

It takes sensor ID as input and returns one data set of
`demo02sensor_active_TS`.

PROCEDURE

```
1.     "DemoSchema"."demoApp.demo01.app02.SHIOT_02.Procedures::se
       nsor_read(
2.
3.     IN id NVARCHAR(10),
4.
5.     OUT result
       "DemoSchema"."demoApp.demo01.app02.SHIOT_02.Data::demo02se
       nsorNetwork.demo02sensor_active_TS")
6.
7.     LANGUAGE SQLSCRIPT
8.
9.     SQL SECURITY INVOKER
10.
11.    --DEFAULT SCHEMA
12.
13.    READS SQL DATA <u>AS</u>
14.
15.    BEGIN
16.
17.    /*****************************
18.
19.    Reading sensors Data
20.
21.    *****************************/
22.
23.    result = select *
24.
25.    from
       "DemoSchema"."demoApp.demo01.app02.SHIOT_02.Data::demo02se
       nsorNetwork.demo02sensor_active_TS"
26.
27.    where "ID" = :id and "time_stamp" = (select
       max("time_stamp") from
28.
29.    "DemoSchema"."demoApp.demo01.app02.SHIOT_02.Data::demo02se
       nsorNetwork.demo02sensor_active_TS"
30.
24.    where "ID"= :id);
```

```
25.    END;
```

Step3: Create the XSJS services

Create the **XSJS services** to act as a Gateway between the SQL Procedures calls and the **service calls for Raspberry Pi and SAP UI5 application**.

We have two services.

The first one is `getSensorReading.xsjs`, which reads the recent sensor reading for the sensor id, passed in the URL.

It uses `sensor_read.hdbprocedure` for database call.

```
1.      var sensorId = $.request.parameters.get("id");
2.
3.      var body = "error";
4.
5.      var data ={
6.
7.      "id":"error",
8.
9.      "timestamp":"error",
10.
11.     "value":0
12.
13.     };
14.
15.     body = sensorId;
16.
17.     if(sensorId === undefined){
18.
19.     $.response.setBody( "Invalid key !!!");
```

```
20.
21.    }
22.
23.    else{
24.
25.    $.response.contentType = "text/plain";
26.
27.    $.response.setBody(sensorId);
28.
29.    try {
30.
31.    var conn = $.db.getConnection();
32.
33.    var query = 'call
       \"demoApp.demo01.app02.SHIOT_02.Procedures::sensor_read\"(
       ?,?)';
34.
35.    var cst = conn.prepareCall(query);
36.
37.    cst.setString(1, sensorId);
38.
39.    var rs = cst.execute();
40.
41.    conn.commit();
42.
43.    rs = cst.getResultSet();
44.
45.    while(rs.next()){
46.
47.    data.id = rs.getNString(1);
48.
49.    data.timestamp= rs.getTimestamp(2) ;
50.
51.    data.value= rs.getInteger(3);
52.
53.    }
54.
55.    body = JSON.stringify(data);
56.
57.    conn.close();
58.
```

```
59.    } catch (e) {
60.
61.    body = e.stack + "\nName:"+ e.name+"\nMsg" + e.message;
62.
63.    $.response.status = $.net.http.BAD_REQUEST;
64.
65.    }
66.
67.    }
68.
69.    $.response.contentType = "text/plain";
70.
71.    $.response.setBody(body);
```

Then after that, we use `putSensorReading.xsjs`, which reads the recent sensor reading for the sensor id and sensor value passed in the URL.

It uses `insert_sensor_reading.hdbprocedure` for database call to store the data.

```
1.     var sensorId = $.request.parameters.get("id");
2.
3.     var sensorReading = $.request.parameters.get("value");
4.
5.     sensorReading = parseInt(sensorReading,10);
6.
7.     var body = "error";
8.
9.     if(sensorId === undefined){
10.
11.    $.response.setBody( "Invalid key !!!");
12.
13.    }
14.
15.    else{
16.
17.    $.response.contentType = "text/plain";
```

```
18.
19.    $.response.setBody(sensorId);
20.
21.    try {
22.
23.    var conn = $.db.getConnection();
24.
25.    var query = 'call
       \"demoApp.demo01.app02.SHIOT_02.Procedures::insert_sensor_
       reading\"(?,?)';
26.
27.    var cst = conn.prepareCall(query);
28.
29.    cst.setString(1, sensorId);
30.
31.    cst.setInteger(2, sensorReading);
32.
33.    var rs = cst.execute();
34.
35.    conn.commit();
36.
37.    //as no record returned
38.
39.    if(rs == 0){
40.
41.    body = true;
42.
43.    }
44.
45.    conn.close();
46.
47.    } catch (e) {
48.
49.    body = e.stack + "\nName:"+ e.name+"\nMsg" + e.message;
50.
51.    $.response.status = $.net.http.BAD_REQUEST;
52.
53.    }
54.
55.    }
56.
```

```
57.    $.response.contentType = "text/plain";
58.
59.    $.response.setBody(body);
```

In the real world setup, we need also to assign the security key to each sensor and pass it to verify the readings.

In addition, it would be better to have the timestamp taken from the sensor source and store it in the database but for keeping the coding and complexity minimum we are focusing on the core steps.

3.7   Setting Up SAPUI5

We will configure now the UI, which is going to show the sensor
information.

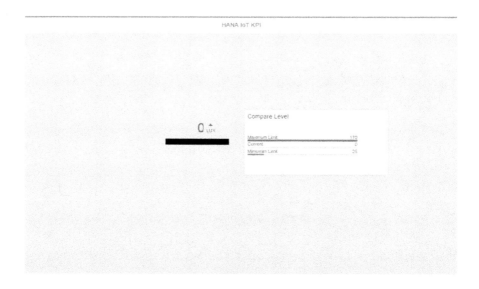

The UI is simple and we have kept two tiles

The first tile is showing the value of the sensor i.e. the LUX value or
light intensity. The small window, below the reading value, tells
how the sensor looks like (used custom CSS mapping).

We are going to create a simple view and controller and place the
tiles in the view. The tiles will be placed in the tile container and the
tile container will be returned inside the content of the page.

There are 3 main components

1. Index.html
2. View
3. Controller

Code for the above components:

Index.html

```
1.    HANA IoT
2.
3.    <script>// <![CDATA[
4.    sap.ui.localResources("shiot_ui"); app = new
      sap.m.App({initialPage:"idshiot_ui1"}); var page =
      sap.ui.view({id:"idshiot_ui1",
      viewName:"shiot_ui_02.shiot_ui_02",
      type:sap.ui.core.mvc.ViewType.JS}); app.addPage(page);
      app.placeAt("content");
5.    // ]]></script>
6.
7.    <div id="splash-screen">
8.    <div class="splash-screen-text">
9.    <div class="en">Welcome to HANA IoT Demo</div>
10.   </div>
11.   <div class="splash-screen-circle-outer"></div>
12.   <div class="splash-screen-circle-inner"></div>
13.   </div>
14.   <script id="sap-ui-bootstrap"
      src="https://sapui5.hana.ondemand.com/resources/sap-ui-
      core.js" data-sap-ui-
      libs="sap.m,sap.suite.ui.commons,sap.ui.core,sap.viz"
      data-sap-ui-theme="sap_bluecrystal">// <![CDATA[
15.
16.   // ]]></script>
```

View

```
1.    sap.ui.jsview("shiot_ui_02.shiot_ui_02", {
2.
3.    /** Specifies the Controller belonging to this View.
4.
5.    * In the case that it is not implemented, or that "null"
      is returned, this View does not have a Controller.
6.
7.    * @memberOf shiot_ui_02.shiot_ui_02
8.
9.    */
10.
11.   getControllerName : function() {
12.
13.   return "shiot_ui_02.shiot_ui_02";
14.
15.   },
16.
17.   /** Is initially called once after the Controller has been
      instantiated. It is the place where the UI is constructed.
18.
19.   * Since the Controller is given to this method, its event
      handlers can be attached right away.
20.
21.   * @memberOf shiot_ui_02.shiot_ui_02
22.
23.   */
24.
25.   createContent : function(oController) {
26.
27.   var content = new
      sap.suite.ui.commons.NumericContent("idInRateValue", {
28.
29.   size: "S",
30.
31.   scale: "LUX",
32.
33.   value: "{/value}",
```

```
34.
35.     valueColor: "Good",
36.
37.     indicator: "{/direction}"
38.
39.     });
40.
41.     var tileContent = new
        sap.suite.ui.commons.TileContent("idInTileCont", {
42.
43.     unit: "",
44.
45.     size: "L",
46.
47.     content: [
48.
49.     content
50.
51.     ]
52.
53.     });
54.
55.     var tileInInfo = new
        sap.suite.ui.commons.GenericTile("idTileInInfo", {
56.
57.     header: "In",
58.
59.     size: "S",
60.
61.     frameType: "TwoByOne",
62.
63.     tileContent: [
64.
65.     tileContent
66.
67.     ]
68.
69.     });
70.
71.     var tileCompr = new
        sap.suite.ui.commons.GenericTile("idAllGTStatus", {
```

```
72.
73.    header: "Compare Level",
74.
75.    size: "L",
76.
77.    scale: "L",
78.
79.    frameType: "TwoByOne",
80.
81.    press: function(){
82.
83.    sap.m.MessageToast.show("Demo");
84.
85.    },
86.
87.    tileContent: [
88.
89.    new sap.suite.ui.commons.TileContent("idDaysComprDash", {
90.
91.    size: "S",
92.
93.    scale: "S",
94.
95.    content: [
96.
97.    new sap.suite.ui.commons.ComparisonChart("idDaysCompr", {
98.
99.    size: "XS",
100.
101.    width: "18rem",
102.
103.    data: [
104.
105.    new sap.suite.ui.commons.ComparisonData({
106.
107.    title: "Maximum Limit",
108.
109.    value: "{/comparisonValue1}",
110.
111.    color: sap.suite.ui.commons.InfoTileValueColor.Error
112.
```

```
113.   }),
114.
115.   new sap.suite.ui.commons.ComparisonData({
116.
117.   title: "Current",
118.
119.   value: "{/comparisonValue2}",
120.
121.   color: sap.suite.ui.commons.InfoTileValueColor.Critical
122.
123.   }),new sap.suite.ui.commons.ComparisonData({
124.
125.   title: "Mimumim Limit",
126.
127.   value: "{/comparisonValue3}",
128.
129.   color: sap.suite.ui.commons.InfoTileValueColor.Good
130.
131.   })
132.
133.   ]
134.
135.   })
136.
137.   ]
138.
139.   })
140.
141.   ]
142.
143.   });
144.
145.   tileCompr.addStyleClass("sapMTile backGroundWhite");
146.
147.   var custeReading = new sap.m.CustomTile({
148.
149.   content: [
150.
151.   tileContent
152.
153.   ]
```

```
154.
155.   });
156.
157.   var custeCompare = new sap.m.CustomTile({
158.
159.   content: [
160.
161.   tileCompr
162.
163.   ]
164.
165.   });
166.
167.   var tileContainer = new sap.m.TileContainer("idMainTiles",
       {
168.
169.   tiles: [
170.
171.   custeReading,
172.
173.   custeCompare
174.
175.   ]
176.
177.   });
178.
179.   //Polling implementation
180.
181.   setInterval(oController.changeKPITest, 1000 * 3);
182.
183.   // create the page holding the List
184.
185.   var page1 = new sap.m.Page({
186.
187.   title: "HANA IoT KPI",
188.
189.   enableScrolling: false,
190.
191.   content : [
192.
193.   tileContainer
```

```
194.
195.    ]
196.
197.    });
198.
199.    return page1;
200.
201.    }

203.    });
```

Controller

```
1.      sap.ui.controller("shiot_ui_02.shiot_ui_02", {
2.
3.      /**
4.
5.      * Called when a controller is instantiated and its View
        controls (if available) are already created.
6.
7.      * Can be used to modify the View before it is displayed,
        to bind event handlers and do other one-time
        initialization.
8.
9.      * @memberOf shiot_ui_02.shiot_ui_02
10.
11.     */
12.
13.     //onInit: function() {
14.
15.     //
16.
17.     //},
18.
19.     /**
20.
21.     * Similar to onAfterRendering, but this hook is invoked
        before the controller's View is re-rendered
22.
23.     * (NOT before the first rendering! onInit() is used for
        that one!).
24.
25.     * @memberOf shiot_ui_02.shiot_ui_02
26.
27.     */
28.
29.     onBeforeRendering: function() {
30.
31.     var data = {
32.
33.     "value": 0,
```

```
34.
35.    "direction": "Down",
36.
37.    "comparisonValue1": 0,
38.
39.    "comparisonValue2": 0,
40.
41.    "comparisonValue3": 0
42.
43.    };
44.
45.    var oModel = new sap.ui.model.json.JSONModel();
46.
47.    oModel.setData(data);
48.
49.    sap.ui.getCore().setModel(oModel);
50.
51.    },
52.
53.    //Triggers automatically for display test
54.
55.    changeKPITest: function(){
56.
57.    /*var min = 0;
58.
59.    var max = 100;
60.
61.    var newRandomreading = Math.floor(Math.random() * (max -
       min)) + min;*/
62.
63.    var url =
       "http:///demoApp/demo01/app01/services/getSensorReading.xs
       js?id=";
64.
65.    var _SENSORID = "A001";
66.
67.    var _MAXLIMIT = 170;
68.
69.    var _MINLIMIT = 25;
70.
71.    var data = {
```

```
72.
73.     "value": 0,
74.
75.     "direction": "Down",
76.
77.     "comparisonValue1": _MAXLIMIT,
78.
79.     "comparisonValue2": 0,
80.
81.     "comparisonValue3": _MINLIMIT
82.
83.     };
84.
85.     var oModel;
86.
87.     var newColorCode;
88.
89.     //for now hardcoding the sensor ID
90.
91.     url = url + _SENSORID;
92.
93.     //Doing the asyn call to HANA system
94.
95.     jQuery.ajax({
96.
97.     url: url,
98.
99.     async: true,
100.
101.    dataType: 'json',
102.
103.    type: 'GET',
104.
105.    success: function(oData) {
106.
107.    if (!oData) {
108.
109.    sap.m.MessageToast.show("Not able to get Data");
110.
111.    } else {
112.
```

```
113.   data["value"] = oData["value"];
114.
115.   data["comparisonValue2"] = oData["value"];
116.
117.   oModel = sap.ui.getCore().getModel();
118.
119.   if(oModel.getData()["comparisonValue2"] >
       data["comparisonValue2"]){
120.
121.   data["direction"] = "Down";
122.
123.   }else{
124.
125.   data["direction"] = "Up";
126.
127.   }
128.
129.   oModel.setData(data);
130.
131.   oModel.refresh();
132.
133.   //changing the color as well
134.
135.   newColorCode = parseInt(data["value"])*2 ;
136.
137.   if(newColorCode > 255){
138.
139.   newColorCode = 255;
140.
141.   }
142.
143.   $('#idInTileCont-footer-text').css("background-color",
       "rgba("+newColorCode+", "+newColorCode+",
       "+newColorCode+", 0.99)");
144.
145.   }
146.
147.   },
148.
149.   error: function(XMLHttpRequest, textStatus, errorThrown) {
150.
```

79

```
151.   sap.m.MessageToast.show("Connection not able to
       establish");
152.
153.   }
154.
155.   });
156.
157.   },
158.
159.   /**
160.
161.   * Called when the View has been rendered (so its HTML is
       part of the document). Post-rendering manipulations of the
       HTML could be done here.
162.
163.   * This hook is the same one that SAPUI5 controls get after
       being rendered.
164.
165.   * @memberOf shiot_ui_02.shiot_ui_02
166.
167.   */
168.
169.   //onAfterRendering: function() {
170.
171.   //
172.
173.   //},
174.
175.   /**
176.
177.   * Called when the Controller is destroyed. Use this one to
       free resources and finalize activities.
178.
179.   * @memberOf shiot_ui_02.shiot_ui_02
180.
181.   */
182.
183.   //onExit: function() {
184.
185.   //
186.
```

```
187.    //}
188.
189.    });
```

Here the controller function **changeKPITest** is polled every 3 sec and we have the new data bound to model, which is returned from SAP HANA XSJS AJAX call.

It is better to have a push notification feature in here instead of polling, which is called web-sockets, but for simplicity purpose, we have kept the configuration minimal.

3.8   Tying Loose Ends and Going Live

All the components are now setup individually and all we need to do is to run them synchronously.

We should double check the URLs of the services that link Raspberry Pi to SAP HANA system, from the sensor side, and SAP HANA system to SAPUI5, from the front end user's side.

Let us go for the go-live for that we are going to open the SAPUI5 app screen and start the Java program that reads the serial data and sends the data back to HANA system.

Now, once we start the Java program, we will instantly see the SAPUI5 app starts updating all the sensors data, on near real time basis.

A video result is shown here:

Congratulations, we have now a working prototype ready of application leveraging Internet of Things with Raspberry Pi, Arduino Uno, sensors, SAP HANA and SAPUI5.

You can also check our SAP HANA Internet of Things(IoT) video course for accelerated learning: here or use the below QR code.

SAP HANA Internet of Things(IoT):Raspberry, Uno, PubNub, UI5

UI5 Community Network • SAP Experts - SAP Services, SAP Consulting, SAP Education

★ ★ ★ ★ ★ 4.2 (40 ratings)   • 29 lectures   • 4.5 hours video   • All Levels

4. Bonus

With all the above steps, we have covered an entire Internet of Things use case with SAP HANA.

The steps involving hardware configuration and integration can be challenging and for that reason, we have compiled this entire series in an easy to understand video course.

The course will give you a 360-degree view on how to work with IoT and giving a glimpse of some already implemented use cases in the marketplace.

You can also check our SAP HANA Internet of Things (IoT) video course for accelerated learning: here or use the below QR code.

REFERENCING AND BIBLIOGRAPHY

- Ida.gov.sg, 'The Internet of Things (IOT)'[Online] Available from], https://www.ida.gov.sg/~/media/Files/Infocomm%20Landscape/Techn ology/TechnologyRoadmap/InternetOfThings.pdf

- Cisco ,'The Internet of Things (IOT)'[Online] Available from] https://www.cisco.com/web/about/ac79/docs/innov/IoT_IBSG_0411FI NAL.pdf

- arduino.cc Example and instruction of Serial communication instruction using Java.

- raspberrypi.org Instruction of using Raspberry Pi and interfacing with other devices.

- gartner.com The Internet of Things (IOT)'[Online] Publicly available estimation figure of Internet of Things.